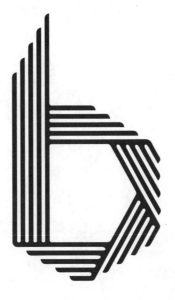

BANDING TOGETHER

"Come, follow me," Jesus said, "and I will send you out to fish for people."

—Mark 1:17

START DATE   END DATE

wesleyan
PUBLISHING HOUSE
wphstore.com
Indianapolis, Indiana

Banding Together: A Practical Guide for Disciple Makers Journal
Copyright © 2018 by Jon Wiest
Published by Wesleyan Publishing House, Indianapolis, Indiana 46250. USA.
ISBN: 978-1-63257-269-1

GUIDE TO DAILY TIME WITH GOD
HOW TO USE THIS JOURNAL

Step 1: *Pause*
Spend a few moments in prayer, asking the Holy Spirit to guide and direct your reading of the Bible. Read with an open heart and listen for any words of direction, encouragement, or correction.

Step 2: *Read*
Go over the reading plan and read the chapters of the Bible listed for that day. While you read, underline or highlight any words, phrases, or verses that you sense God is speaking to you about.

Step 3: *Write*
Turn to a fresh page in your journal, write the date and page number at the top, and then go through the four-step process of journaling to reflect your thoughts.

- **First,** write out the verse or passage of Scripture that the Holy Spirit has shown you for that day. Include the reference.

- **Second,** look at the surrounding context of the verse you selected and write down any observations. Try to explain the passage in your own words.

- **Third,** ask how this verse might apply to your life. What is God calling you to do or to remember as a result? What is your next step and how can you be obedient?

- **Fourth,** write out a closing prayer. Use this final section to speak back to God a request or commitment.

Finish your journal entry by giving it a short title at the top and then transfer the date, Scripture reference, title, and page number to the table of contents.

Step 4: *Review*
When you finish your journal entry, review the accountability questions from the Discipleship Group Agenda, located on the inside front cover.

Step 5: *Pray*
Conclude your time by praying for what you have written and for anyone who needs to surrender to God.

1/25	*"Be A Witness"*	*Acts 1:8*
DATE	TITLE	SCRIPTURE

WRITE OUT THE SCRIPTURE PASSAGE

But you will receive power when the Holy Spirit comes on you; and you will be my witnesses in Jerusalem, and in all Judea and Samaria, and to the ends of the earth (Acts 1:8).

MAKE OBSERVATIONS

Jesus is speaking to his apostles in this verse and telling them that it is the Holy Spirit who will empower them. He will help them become better witnesses. There are three distinct places he is asking his followers to go.

APPLY TO YOUR LIFE

I need to be a better witness. I do a pretty good job sharing my faith with my immediate family and neighbors, but it's harder for me to be a witness for Jesus at work and with my extended family. I need to pray for the Holy Spirit to make me a better witness.

WRITE OUT A PRAYER

Dear Jesus, empower me with boldness today! I want to be a better witness for you. Give me an opportunity to share my faith today with those around me. Amen.

How will I be different today because of what I have read?

TABLE OF CONTENTS

TABLE OF CONTENTS

TABLE OF CONTENTS

DATE	SCRIPTURE	TITLE	PAGE #

TABLE OF CONTENTS

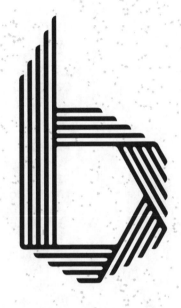

READING PLAN

By following this plan, you will read through
the New Testament, Psalms, and Proverbs
once a year. In the summer, choose one of the
provided options from the Old Testament to
complete that reading every four years.

JANUARY

1 ☐ Luke 1
2 ☐ Luke 2
3 ☐ Luke 3; Ps. 1
4 ☐ Luke 4
5 ☐ Luke 5; Ps. 2
6 ☐ Luke 6
7 ☐ Luke 7
8 ☐ Luke 8
9 ☐ Luke 9
10 ☐ Luke 10
11 ☐ Luke 11
12 ☐ Luke 12
13 ☐ Luke 13; Ps. 3
14 ☐ Luke 14; Ps. 4
15 ☐ Luke 15; Ps. 5
16 ☐ Luke 16; Ps. 6
17 ☐ Luke 17; Ps. 7
18 ☐ Luke 18
19 ☐ Luke 19
20 ☐ Luke 20
21 ☐ Luke 21; Ps. 8
22 ☐ Luke 22
23 ☐ Luke 23
24 ☐ Luke 24
25 ☐ Acts 1; Ps. 9
26 ☐ Acts 2
27 ☐ Acts 3; Ps. 10
28 ☐ Acts 4; Ps. 11
29 ☐ Acts 5
30 ☐ Acts 6; Ps. 12
31 ☐ Review

FEBRUARY

1 ☐ Acts 7; Ps. 13
2 ☐ Acts 8
3 ☐ Acts 9
4 ☐ Acts 10
5 ☐ Acts 11; Ps. 14
6 ☐ Acts 12; Ps. 15
7 ☐ Acts 13
8 ☐ Acts 14; Ps. 16
9 ☐ Acts 15
10 ☐ Acts 16
11 ☐ Acts 17; Ps. 17
12 ☐ Acts 18; Ps. 18: 1–19
13 ☐ Acts 19; Ps. 18:20–50
14 ☐ Acts 20; Ps. 19

15 ☐ Acts 21
16 ☐ Acts 22; Ps. 20
17 ☐ Acts 23; Ps. 21
18 ☐ Acts 24; Ps. 22:1–18
19 ☐ Acts 25; Ps. 22:19–31
20 ☐ Acts 26; Ps. 23
21 ☐ Acts 27; Ps. 24
22 ☐ Acts 28; Ps. 25
23 ☐ Gal. 1; Ps. 26
24 ☐ Gal. 2; Ps. 27
25 ☐ Gal. 3; Ps. 28
26 ☐ Gal. 4; Ps. 29
27 ☐ Gal. 5; Ps. 30
28 ☐ Review
29 ☐ Review

MARCH

1 ☐ Gal. 6; Ps. 31
2 ☐ 1 Cor. 1; Ps. 32
3 ☐ 1 Cor. 2; Ps. 33
4 ☐ 1 Cor. 3; Ps. 34
5 ☐ 1 Cor. 4; Ps. 35
6 ☐ 1 Cor. 5; Ps. 36
7 ☐ 1 Cor. 6; Ps. 37:1–22
8 ☐ 1 Cor. 7
9 ☐ 1 Cor. 8; Ps. 37:23–40
10 ☐ 1 Cor. 9; Ps. 38
11 ☐ 1 Cor. 10; Ps. 39
12 ☐ 1 Cor. 11; Ps. 40
13 ☐ 1 Cor. 12; Ps. 41
14 ☐ 1 Cor. 13; Ps. 42
15 ☐ 1 Cor. 14
16 ☐ 1 Cor. 15
17 ☐ 1 Cor. 16; Ps. 43
18 ☐ 2 Cor. 1; Ps. 44
19 ☐ 2 Cor. 2; Ps. 45
20 ☐ 2 Cor. 3; Ps. 46
21 ☐ 2 Cor. 4; Ps. 47
22 ☐ 2 Cor. 5; Ps. 48
23 ☐ 2 Cor. 6; Ps. 49
24 ☐ 2 Cor. 7; Ps. 50
25 ☐ 2 Cor. 8; Ps. 51
26 ☐ 2 Cor. 9; Ps. 52
27 ☐ 2 Cor. 10; Ps. 53
28 ☐ 2 Cor. 11; Ps. 54
29 ☐ 2 Cor. 12; Ps. 55
30 ☐ 2 Cor. 13
31 ☐ Review

APRIL

1 ☐ Mark 1; Ps. 56
2 ☐ Mark 2; Ps. 57
3 ☐ Mark 3; Ps. 58
4 ☐ Mark 4–5
5 ☐ Mark 6; Ps. 59
6 ☐ Mark 7; Ps. 60
7 ☐ Mark 8; Ps. 61
8 ☐ Mark 9
9 ☐ Mark 10; Ps. 62
10 ☐ Mark 11; Ps. 63
11 ☐ Mark 12
12 ☐ Mark 13; Ps. 64
13 ☐ Mark 14; Ps. 65
14 ☐ Mark 15
15 ☐ Mark 16; Ps. 66
16 ☐ 1 Thess. 1; Ps. 67
17 ☐ 1 Thess. 2; Ps. 68:1–18
18 ☐ 1 Thess. 3; Ps. 68:19–35
19 ☐ 1 Thess. 4; Ps. 69:1–16
20 ☐ 1 Thess. 5; Ps. 69:17–36
21 ☐ 2 Thess. 1; Ps. 70
22 ☐ 2 Thess. 2; Ps. 71
23 ☐ 2 Thess. 3; Ps. 72
24 ☐ Rom. 1; Ps. 73:1–15
25 ☐ Rom. 2; Ps. 73:16–28
26 ☐ Rom. 3; Ps. 74
27 ☐ Rom. 4; Ps. 75
28 ☐ Rom. 5; Ps. 76
29 ☐ Rom. 6; Ps. 77
30 ☐ Review

MAY

1 ☐ Rom. 7; Ps. 78:1–20
2 ☐ Rom. 8; Ps. 78:21–55
3 ☐ Rom. 9; Ps. 78:56–72
4 ☐ Rom. 10; Ps. 79
5 ☐ Rom. 11; Ps. 80
6 ☐ Rom. 12; Ps. 81
7 ☐ Rom. 13; Ps. 82
8 ☐ Rom. 14; Ps. 83
9 ☐ Rom. 15; Ps. 84
10 ☐ Rom. 16; Ps. 85
11 ☐ Eph. 1; Ps. 86
12 ☐ Eph. 2; Ps. 87
13 ☐ Eph. 3; Ps. 88
14 ☐ Eph. 4; Ps. 89:1–18
15 ☐ Eph. 5; Ps. 89:19–35

16 ☐ Eph. 6; Ps. 89:36–52
17 ☐ Phil. 1; Ps. 90
18 ☐ Phil. 2; Ps. 91
19 ☐ Phil. 3; Ps. 92
20 ☐ Phil. 4; Ps. 93
21 ☐ Col. 1; Ps. 94
22 ☐ Col. 2; Ps. 95
23 ☐ Col. 3; Ps. 96
24 ☐ Col. 4; Ps. 97
25 ☐ 1 Tim. 1; Ps. 98
26 ☐ 1 Tim. 2; Ps. 99
27 ☐ 1 Tim. 3; Ps. 100
28 ☐ 1 Tim. 4; Ps. 101
29 ☐ 1 Tim. 5; Ps. 102
30 ☐ 1 Tim. 6; Ps. 103
31 ☐ Review

SEPTEMBER

1 ☐ Matt. 1; Ps. 104:1–18
2 ☐ Matt. 2; Ps. 104:19–35
3 ☐ Matt. 3; Ps. 105:1–22
4 ☐ Matt. 4; Ps. 105:23–45
5 ☐ Matt. 5
6 ☐ Matt. 6; Ps. 106:1–12
7 ☐ Matt. 7; Ps. 106:13–48
8 ☐ Matt. 8; Ps. 107:1–22
9 ☐ Matt. 9; Ps. 107:23–43
10 ☐ Matt. 10
11 ☐ Matt. 11; Ps. 108
12 ☐ Matt. 12
13 ☐ Matt. 13
14 ☐ Matt. 14; Ps. 109:1–20
15 ☐ Matt. 15; Ps. 109:21–31
16 ☐ Matt. 16; Ps. 110
17 ☐ Matt. 17; Ps. 111
18 ☐ Matt. 18; Ps. 112
19 ☐ Matt. 19; Ps. 113
20 ☐ Matt. 20; Ps. 114
21 ☐ Matt. 21
22 ☐ Matt. 22
23 ☐ Matt. 23; Ps. 115
24 ☐ Matt. 24
25 ☐ Matt. 25
26 ☐ Matt. 26
27 ☐ Matt. 27
28 ☐ Matt. 28; Ps. 116
29 ☐ 2 Tim. 1; Ps. 117
30 ☐ Review

OCTOBER

1 ☐ 2 Tim. 2; Ps. 118
2 ☐ 2 Tim. 3; Ps. 119:1–24
3 ☐ 2 Tim. 4; Ps. 119:25–56
4 ☐ Titus 1; Ps. 119:57–80
5 ☐ Titus 2; Ps. 119:81–104
6 ☐ Titus 3; Ps. 119:105–136
7 ☐ Phile.; Ps. 119:137–160
8 ☐ Heb. 1; Ps. 119:161–176
9 ☐ Heb. 2; Ps. 120
10 ☐ Heb. 3; Ps. 121
11 ☐ Heb. 4; Ps. 122
12 ☐ Heb. 5; Ps. 123
13 ☐ Heb. 6; Ps. 124
14 ☐ Heb. 7; Ps. 125
15 ☐ Heb. 8; Ps. 126
16 ☐ Heb. 9; Ps. 127
17 ☐ Heb. 10; Ps. 128
18 ☐ Heb. 11
19 ☐ Heb. 12; Ps. 129
20 ☐ Heb. 13; Ps. 130
21 ☐ James 1; Ps. 131
22 ☐ James 2; Ps. 132
23 ☐ James 3; Ps. 133
24 ☐ James 4; Ps. 134
25 ☐ James 5; Ps. 135
26 ☐ 1 Pet. 1; Ps. 136
27 ☐ 1 Pet. 2; Ps. 137
28 ☐ 1 Pet. 3; Ps. 138
29 ☐ 1 Pet. 4; Ps. 139
30 ☐ 1 Pet. 5; Ps. 140
31 ☐ Review

NOVEMBER

1 ☐ 2 Pet. 1; Ps. 141
2 ☐ 2 Pet. 2; Ps. 142
3 ☐ 2 Pet. 3; Ps. 143
4 ☐ John 1
5 ☐ John 2; Ps. 144
6 ☐ John 3; Ps. 145
7 ☐ John 4
8 ☐ John 5
9 ☐ John 6
10 ☐ John 7
11 ☐ John 8
12 ☐ John 9
13 ☐ John 10
14 ☐ John 11
15 ☐ John 12
16 ☐ John 13; Ps. 146
17 ☐ John 14; Ps. 147
18 ☐ John 15; Ps. 148
19 ☐ John 16; Ps. 149
20 ☐ John 17; Ps. 150
21 ☐ John 18
22 ☐ John 19
23 ☐ John 20; Prov. 1
24 ☐ John 21; Prov. 2
25 ☐ 1 John 1; Prov. 3
26 ☐ 1 John 2; Prov. 4
27 ☐ 1 John 3; Prov. 5
28 ☐ 1 John 4; Prov. 6
29 ☐ 1 John 5; Prov. 7
30 ☐ Review

DECEMBER

1 ☐ 2 John; 3 John; Prov. 8
2 ☐ Jude; Prov. 9
3 ☐ Rev. 1; Prov. 10
4 ☐ Rev. 2; Prov. 11
5 ☐ Rev. 3; Prov. 12
6 ☐ Rev. 4; Prov. 13
7 ☐ Rev. 5; Prov. 14
8 ☐ Rev. 6; Prov. 15
9 ☐ Rev. 7; Prov. 16
10 ☐ Rev. 8; Prov. 17
11 ☐ Rev. 9; Prov. 18
12 ☐ Rev. 10; Prov. 19
13 ☐ Rev. 11; Prov. 20
14 ☐ Rev. 12; Prov. 21
15 ☐ Rev. 13; Prov. 22
16 ☐ Rev. 14; Prov. 23
17 ☐ Rev. 15; Prov. 24
18 ☐ Rev. 16; Prov. 25
19 ☐ Rev. 17; Prov. 26
20 ☐ Rev. 18; Prov. 27
21 ☐ Rev. 19; Prov. 28
22 ☐ Rev. 20; Prov. 29
23 ☐ Rev. 21; Prov. 30
24 ☐ Rev. 22; Prov. 31
25 ☐ Year Review Week
26 ☐ Year Review Week
27 ☐ Year Review Week
28 ☐ Year Review Week
29 ☐ Year Review Week
30 ☐ Year Review Week
31 ☐ Year Review Week

OLD TESTAMENT OPTION ONE: THE LAW

JUNE

1 ☐ Gen. 1–2
2 ☐ Gen. 3–4
3 ☐ Gen. 5–6
4 ☐ Gen. 7–8
5 ☐ Gen. 9–10
6 ☐ Gen. 11–12
7 ☐ Gen. 13–14
8 ☐ Gen. 15–16
9 ☐ Gen. 17–18
10 ☐ Gen. 19–20
11 ☐ Gen. 21–23
12 ☐ Gen. 24
13 ☐ Gen. 25–26
14 ☐ Gen. 27
15 ☐ Gen. 28–29
16 ☐ Gen. 30
17 ☐ Gen. 31
18 ☐ Gen. 32–33
19 ☐ Gen. 34–35
20 ☐ Gen. 36–37
21 ☐ Gen. 38
22 ☐ Gen. 39
23 ☐ Gen. 40–41
24 ☐ Gen. 42
25 ☐ Gen. 43–44
26 ☐ Gen. 45–46
27 ☐ Gen. 47–48
28 ☐ Gen. 49
29 ☐ Gen. 50
30 ☐ Review

JULY

1 ☐ Ex. 1–2
2 ☐ Ex. 3–4
3 ☐ Ex. 5–6
4 ☐ Ex. 7–8
5 ☐ Ex. 9–10
6 ☐ Ex. 11–12
7 ☐ Ex. 13–14
8 ☐ Ex. 15–16
9 ☐ Ex. 17–18
10 ☐ Ex. 19–20
11 ☐ Ex. 21–22
12 ☐ Ex. 23–24
13 ☐ Ex. 25–26
14 ☐ Ex. 27–28
15 ☐ Ex. 29–30
16 ☐ Ex. 31–32
17 ☐ Ex. 33–34
18 ☐ Ex. 35–36
19 ☐ Ex. 37–38
20 ☐ Ex. 39–40
21 ☐ Lev. 1–3
22 ☐ Lev. 4–5
23 ☐ Lev. 6–7
24 ☐ Lev. 8
25 ☐ Lev. 9–10
26 ☐ Lev. 16–17
27 ☐ Lev. 18–19
28 ☐ Lev. 20–21
29 ☐ Lev. 22–23
30 ☐ Lev. 24
31 ☐ Review

AUGUST

1 ☐ Lev. 25–26
2 ☐ Lev. 27
3 ☐ Num. 1–2
4 ☐ Num. 3–4
5 ☐ Num. 5–6
6 ☐ Num. 7–8
7 ☐ Num. 9–10
8 ☐ Num. 11–12
9 ☐ Num. 13–14
10 ☐ Num. 15–16
11 ☐ Num. 17–18
12 ☐ Num. 19–20
13 ☐ Num. 21–22
14 ☐ Num. 23–24
15 ☐ Num. 25–26
16 ☐ Num. 27–28
17 ☐ Num. 29–30
18 ☐ Num. 31–32
19 ☐ Num. 33–34
20 ☐ Num. 35–36
21 ☐ Deut. 1–3
22 ☐ Deut. 4–5
23 ☐ Deut. 6–7
24 ☐ Deut. 8–9
25 ☐ Deut. 10–11
26 ☐ Deut. 26–27
27 ☐ Deut. 28–29
28 ☐ Deut. 30–31
29 ☐ Deut. 32–33
30 ☐ Deut. 34
31 ☐ Review

OLD TESTAMENT OPTION TWO: HISTORY

JUNE

1 ☐ Josh. 1–2
2 ☐ Josh. 3–4
3 ☐ Josh. 5–6
4 ☐ Josh. 7–8
5 ☐ Josh. 9–10
6 ☐ Josh. 11–12
7 ☐ Josh. 22–23
8 ☐ Josh. 24
9 ☐ Judg. 1
10 ☐ Judg. 2–3
11 ☐ Judg. 4–5
12 ☐ Judg. 6–7
13 ☐ Judg. 8
14 ☐ Judg. 9
15 ☐ Judg. 10–12
16 ☐ Judg. 13–14
17 ☐ Judg. 15–16
18 ☐ Judg. 17–19
19 ☐ Judg. 20–21
20 ☐ Ruth 1–2
21 ☐ Ruth 3–4
22 ☐ 1 Sam. 1–2
23 ☐ 1 Sam. 3–4
24 ☐ 1 Sam. 5–7
25 ☐ 1 Sam. 8–9
26 ☐ 1 Sam. 10–11
27 ☐ 1 Sam. 12–13
28 ☐ 1 Sam. 14
29 ☐ 1 Sam. 15–16
30 ☐ 1 Sam. 17

JULY

1 ☐ 1 Sam. 18–19
2 ☐ 1 Sam. 20
3 ☐ 1 Sam. 21–22
4 ☐ 1 Sam. 23–24
5 ☐ 1 Sam. 25
6 ☐ 1 Sam. 26–27
7 ☐ 1 Sam. 28–29
8 ☐ 1 Sam. 30–31
9 ☐ 2 Sam. 1–2
10 ☐ 2 Sam. 3–4
11 ☐ 2 Sam. 5–6
12 ☐ 2 Sam. 7–8
13 ☐ 2 Sam. 9–11
14 ☐ 2 Sam. 12–13
15 ☐ 2 Sam. 14–15
16 ☐ 2 Sam. 16–17
17 ☐ 2 Sam. 18–19
18 ☐ 2 Sam. 20–21
19 ☐ 2 Sam. 22
20 ☐ 2 Sam. 23–24
21 ☐ 1 Kings 1–2
22 ☐ 1 Kings 3–4
23 ☐ 1 Kings 5–6
24 ☐ 1 Kings 7
25 ☐ 1 Kings 8
26 ☐ 1 Kings 9–10
27 ☐ 1 Kings 11
28 ☐ 1 Kings 12–13
29 ☐ 1 Kings 14–15
30 ☐ 1 Kings 16–17
31 ☐ 1 Kings 18

AUGUST

1 ☐ 1 Kings 19–20
2 ☐ 1 Kings 21–22
3 ☐ 2 Kings 1–2
4 ☐ 2 Kings 3–4
5 ☐ 2 Kings 5–6
6 ☐ 2 Kings 7–8
7 ☐ 2 Kings 9–10
8 ☐ 2 Kings 11–12
9 ☐ 2 Kings 13–14
10 ☐ 2 Kings 15–16
11 ☐ 2 Kings 17–18
12 ☐ 2 Kings 19–20
13 ☐ 2 Kings 21–22
14 ☐ 2 Kings 23
15 ☐ 2 Kings 24
16 ☐ Ezra 1–2
17 ☐ Ezra 3–4
18 ☐ Ezra 5–6
19 ☐ Ezra 7–8
20 ☐ Ezra 9–10
21 ☐ Neh. 1–2
22 ☐ Neh. 3–4
23 ☐ Neh. 5–6
24 ☐ Neh. 7–8
25 ☐ Neh. 9–10
26 ☐ Neh. 11–12
27 ☐ Neh. 13–14
28 ☐ Est. 1–2
29 ☐ Est. 3–5
30 ☐ Est. 6–8
31 ☐ Est. 9–10

OLD TESTAMENT OPTION THREE: PROPHETS

JUNE

1 ☐ Isa. 1–2
2 ☐ Isa. 3–4
3 ☐ Isa. 5–6
4 ☐ Isa. 7–8
5 ☐ Isa. 9–10
6 ☐ Isa. 11–13
7 ☐ Isa. 14–15
8 ☐ Isa. 16–18
9 ☐ Isa. 19–21
10 ☐ Isa. 22–23
11 ☐ Isa. 24–26
12 ☐ Isa. 27–28
13 ☐ Isa. 29–30
14 ☐ Isa. 31–33
15 ☐ Isa. 34–36
16 ☐ Isa. 37–38
17 ☐ Isa. 39–40
18 ☐ Isa. 41–42
19 ☐ Isa. 43–44
20 ☐ Isa. 45–47
21 ☐ Isa. 48–49
22 ☐ Isa. 50–52
23 ☐ Isa. 53–55
24 ☐ Isa. 56–58
25 ☐ Isa. 59–60
26 ☐ Isa. 61–63
27 ☐ Isa. 64–66
28 ☐ Jer. 1–2
29 ☐ Jer. 3–4
30 ☐ Review

JULY

1 ☐ Jer. 5–6
2 ☐ Jer. 7–8
3 ☐ Jer. 9–10
4 ☐ Jer. 11–12
5 ☐ Jer. 13–14
6 ☐ Jer. 15–16
7 ☐ Jer. 17–18
8 ☐ Jer. 19–21
9 ☐ Jer. 22–23
10 ☐ Jer. 24–25
11 ☐ Jer. 26–27
12 ☐ Jer. 28–29
13 ☐ Jer. 30–31
14 ☐ Jer. 32
15 ☐ Jer. 33–34
16 ☐ Jer. 35–36
17 ☐ Jer. 37–38
18 ☐ Jer. 39–40
19 ☐ Jer. 41–42
20 ☐ Jer. 43–44
21 ☐ Jer. 45–47
22 ☐ Jer. 48–49
23 ☐ Jer. 50
24 ☐ Jer. 51
25 ☐ Jer. 52
26 ☐ Lam. 1–2
27 ☐ Lam. 3
28 ☐ Lam. 4–5
29 ☐ Ezek. 1–2
30 ☐ Ezek. 3–4
31 ☐ Review

AUGUST

1 ☐ Ezek. 5–7
2 ☐ Ezek. 8–10
3 ☐ Ezek. 11–12
4 ☐ Ezek. 13–14
5 ☐ Ezek. 15–16
6 ☐ Ezek. 17–18
7 ☐ Ezek. 19–20
8 ☐ Ezek. 21–22
9 ☐ Ezek. 23
10 ☐ Ezek. 24–25
11 ☐ Ezek. 26
12 ☐ Ezek. 27
13 ☐ Ezek. 28–29
14 ☐ Ezek. 30–31
15 ☐ Ezek. 32–33
16 ☐ Ezek. 34–35
17 ☐ Ezek. 36–37
18 ☐ Ezek. 38–39
19 ☐ Ezek. 40
20 ☐ Ezek. 41–42
21 ☐ Ezek. 43–44
22 ☐ Ezek. 45–46
23 ☐ Ezek. 47–48
24 ☐ Dan. 1
25 ☐ Dan. 2
26 ☐ Dan. 3–4
27 ☐ Dan. 5–6
28 ☐ Dan. 7–8
29 ☐ Dan. 9–10
30 ☐ Dan. 11–12
31 ☐ Review

OLD TESTAMENT OPTION FOUR: POETRY/MINOR PROPHETS

JUNE

1 ☐ Job 1–2
2 ☐ Job 3–4
3 ☐ Job 5–6
4 ☐ Job 7–8
5 ☐ Job 9–10
6 ☐ Job 11–12
7 ☐ Job 13–14
8 ☐ Job 15–16
9 ☐ Job 17–18
10 ☐ Job 19–20
11 ☐ Job 21–22
12 ☐ Job 23–24
13 ☐ Job 25–26
14 ☐ Job 27–28
15 ☐ Job 29–30
16 ☐ Job 31–32
17 ☐ Job 33–34
18 ☐ Job 35–36
19 ☐ Job 37–38
20 ☐ Job 39–40
21 ☐ Job 41–42
22 ☐ Prov. 1
23 ☐ Prov. 2
24 ☐ Prov. 3
25 ☐ Prov. 4
26 ☐ Prov. 5
27 ☐ Prov. 6
28 ☐ Prov. 7
29 ☐ Prov. 8
30 ☐ Review

JULY

1 ☐ Prov. 9
2 ☐ Prov. 10
3 ☐ Prov. 11
4 ☐ Prov. 12
5 ☐ Prov. 13
6 ☐ Prov. 14
7 ☐ Prov. 15
8 ☐ Prov. 16
9 ☐ Prov. 17
10 ☐ Prov. 18
11 ☐ Prov. 19
12 ☐ Prov. 20
13 ☐ Prov. 21
14 ☐ Prov. 22
15 ☐ Prov. 23
16 ☐ Prov. 24

17 ☐ Prov. 25
18 ☐ Prov. 26
19 ☐ Prov. 27
20 ☐ Prov. 28
21 ☐ Prov. 29
22 ☐ Prov. 30
23 ☐ Prov. 31
24 ☐ Eccl. 1–3
25 ☐ Eccl. 4–6
26 ☐ Eccl. 7–9
27 ☐ Eccl. 10–12
28 ☐ Song 1–3
29 ☐ Song 4–6
30 ☐ Song 7–8
31 ☐ Review

AUGUST

1 ☐ Hos. 1–2
2 ☐ Hos. 3–5
3 ☐ Hos. 6–8
4 ☐ Hos. 9–11
5 ☐ Hos. 12–14
6 ☐ Joel 1
7 ☐ Joel 2
8 ☐ Joel 3
9 ☐ Amos 1–2
10 ☐ Amos 3–4
11 ☐ Amos 5–6
12 ☐ Amos 7–8
13 ☐ Amos 9
14 ☐ Obad.
15 ☐ Jon. 1–2
16 ☐ Jon. 3–4
17 ☐ Mic. 1–2
18 ☐ Mic. 3–4
19 ☐ Mic. 5–7
20 ☐ Nah. 1–3
21 ☐ Hab. 1–3
22 ☐ Zeph. 1–2
23 ☐ Hag. 1–2
24 ☐ Zech. 1–3
25 ☐ Zech. 4–6
26 ☐ Zech. 7–9
27 ☐ Zech. 10–12
28 ☐ Zech. 13–14
29 ☐ Mal. 1–2
30 ☐ Mal. 3–4
31 ☐ Review

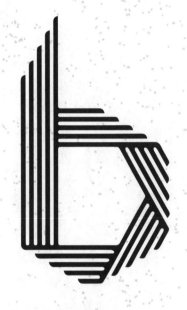

DAILY PAGES

How will I be different today
because of what I have read?

How will I be different today because of what I have read?

DATE | TITLE | SCRIPTURE

How will I be different today because of what I have read?

19

How will I be different today because of what I have read?

How will I be different today because of what I have read?

How will I be different today because of what I have read?

How will I be different today because of what I have read?

How will I be different today because of what I have read?

How will I be different today because of what I have read?

How will I be different today because of what I have read?

How will I be different today because of what I have read?

How will I be different today because of what I have read?

How will I be different today because of what I have read?

How will I be different today because of what I have read?

How will I be different today because of what I have read?

How will I be different today because of what I have read?

How will I be different today because of what I have read?

How will I be different today because of what I have read?

How will I be different today because of what I have read?

How will I be different today because of what I have read?   41

How will I be different today because of what I have read?

How will I be different today because of what I have read?

How will I be different today because of what I have read?

How will I be different today because of what I have read?

How will I be different today because of what I have read?

How will I be different today because of what I have read?

DATE	TITLE	SCRIPTURE

How will I be different today because of what I have read?

How will I be different today because of what I have read?

How will I be different today because of what I have read?

How will I be different today because of what I have read?

How will I be different today because of what I have read?

How will I be different today because of what I have read?

How will I be different today because of what I have read?

How will I be different today because of what I have read?

How will I be different today because of what I have read?

DATE	TITLE	SCRIPTURE

How will I be different today because of what I have read?

How will I be different today because of what I have read?

How will I be different today because of what I have read?

How will I be different today because of what I have read?

How will I be different today because of what I have read?

How will I be different today because of what I have read?

How will I be different today because of what I have read?

How will I be different today because of what I have read?

How will I be different today because of what I have read?

How will I be different today because of what I have read?

How will I be different today because of what I have read?

How will I be different today because of what I have read?

How will I be different today because of what I have read?

How will I be different today because of what I have read?

How will I be different today because of what I have read?

How will I be different today because of what I have read?

How will I be different today because of what I have read?

How will I be different today because of what I have read?

How will I be different today because of what I have read?

How will I be different today because of what I have read?

How will I be different today because of what I have read?

How will I be different today because of what I have read?

How will I be different today because of what I have read?

How will I be different today because of what I have read?

How will I be different today because of what I have read?

How will I be different today because of what I have read?

TITLE   SCRIPTURE

How will I be different today because of what I have read?

How will I be different today because of what I have read?

How will I be different today because of what I have read?

How will I be different today because of what I have read?

How will I be different today because of what I have read?

How will I be different today because of what I have read?

How will I be different today because of what I have read?

How will I be different today because of what I have read?

How will I be different today because of what I have read?

How will I be different today because of what I have read?

How will I be different today because of what I have read?

DATE	TITLE	SCRIPTURE

How will I be different today because of what I have read?

How will I be different today because of what I have read?

How will I be different today because of what I have read?

How will I be different today because of what I have read?

How will I be different today because of what I have read?

How will I be different today because of what I have read?

How will I be different today because of what I have read?

How will I be different today because of what I have read?

How will I be different today because of what I have read?

How will I be different today because of what I have read?

How will I be different today because of what I have read?

DATE	TITLE	SCRIPTURE

How will I be different today because of what I have read?

How will I be different today because of what I have read?

How will I be different today because of what I have read?

How will I be different today because of what I have read?

How will I be different today because of what I have read?

How will I be different today because of what I have read?

How will I be different today because of what I have read?

How will I be different today because of what I have read?

How will I be different today because of what I have read?

How will I be different today because of what I have read?   133

How will I be different today because of what I have read?

How will I be different today because of what I have read?

How will I be different today because of what I have read?

How will I be different today because of what I have read?

How will I be different today because of what I have read?

How will I be different today because of what I have read?

How will I be different today because of what I have read?

DATE	TITLE	SCRIPTURE

How will I be different today because of what I have read?

How will I be different today because of what I have read?

How will I be different today because of what I have read?

How will I be different today because of what I have read?

How will I be different today because of what I have read?

How will I be different today because of what I have read?

How will I be different today because of what I have read?

DATE	TITLE	SCRIPTURE

How will I be different today because of what I have read?

How will I be different today because of what I have read?

DATE	TITLE	SCRIPTURE

How will I be different today because of what I have read?

How will I be different today because of what I have read?

DATE	TITLE	SCRIPTURE

How will I be different today because of what I have read?

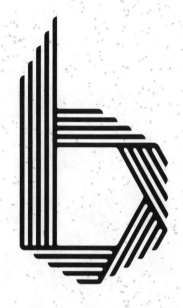

PRAYER LIST

"I tell you that in the same way there will be more rejoicing in heaven over one sinner who repents than over ninety-nine righteous persons who do not need to repent."

—Luke 15:7

PRAYER LIST

DATE	PRAYER	ANSWERED

PRAYER LIST

DATE	PRAYER	ANSWERED

PRAYER LIST

DATE	PRAYER	ANSWERED

PRAYER LIST

DATE	PRAYER	ANSWERED

PRAYER LIST

DATE	PRAYER	ANSWERED